Now You Know
Extreme Weather

Now You Know
Extreme Weather

DOUG LENNOX

THE DUNDURN GROUP
TORONTO

Editor: Nigel Heseltine
Copy editor: Andrea Waters
Design: Alison Carr
Printer: Webcom

**Library and Archives Canada
Cataloguing in Publication**
Lennox, Doug
    Now you know extreme weather /
Doug Lennox.

ISBN 978-1-55002-743-3

    1. Weather--Miscellanea. 2.
Meteorology--Miscellanea.
I. Title.

QC981.L46 2007   551.5
C2007-903566-3

        1   2   3   4   5
    11   10   09   08   07

**Conseil des Arts
du Canada**   **Canada Council
for the Arts**

**ONTARIO ARTS COUNCIL
CONSEIL DES ARTS DE L'ONTARIO**
an Ontario government agency | un organisme du gouvernement de l'Ontario

Canada

We acknowledge the support of
The Canada Council for the Arts
and the **Ontario Arts Council** for
our publishing program. We also
acknowledge the financial support
of the Government of Canada
through the Book Publishing
Industry Development Program and
**The Association for the Export of
Canadian Books**, and the Government
of Ontario through the **Ontario Book
Publishers Tax Credit** program, and
the **Ontario Media Development
Corporation**.

www.dundurn.com

Dundurn Press
3 Church Street, Suite 500
Toronto, Ontario, Canada
M5E 1M2

Gazelle Book Services Ltd.
White Cross Mills
High Town, Lancaster,
England LA1 4XS

Dundurn Press
2250 Military Road
Tonawanda, NY
U.S.A. 14150

Now You Know Extreme Weather

CONTENTS

PREFACE

Weather has been surprising us with its violence, intensity, and beauty since humans first walked the planet. These pages are chock full of examples of weather events that have tested us to our limits and beyond. Questions about changes to long-term weather — the global climate — are addressed as well, because it may be gearing up to take us on a ride into extremes of weather we never dreamed of before.

Many enticing bits of information have been packed into the answers to these questions. I hope they will entertain, intrigue, and motivate you as they have done me.

COLD

What was happening when the highest air pressure record was set?

Tonsontsengel, Mongolia, was in the grip of -40°F (-40°C) temperatures when it dethroned Agata, Siberia, with a barometric reading of 1085.7 millibars, or 32.06 inches (81.4 centimetres) of mercury, on December 19, 2001. Agata's reading of 1083 millibars was also set in bitter cold.

What is the coldest temperature ever recorded in Canada once windchill was taken into account?

This controversial measurement, first developed in 1939, gave Pelly Bay, Nunavut, a reading of -133.6°F (-92°C) on January 13, 1975, when -60°F (-51°C) temperatures combined with 35-mile-per-hour (56-kilometre-per-hour) winds. Recent changes to how windchill is calculated raise this temperature considerably, to -106.6°F (-77°C).

The most extreme windchill readings are found in Antarctica.

Where was the world's fastest temperature drop recorded?

In Rapid City, South Dakota, the temperature fell from 62°F (16.5°C) to -13°F (-25°C) in two hours on January 10, 1911.

How does altitude make a difference?

Flagstaff, Arizona, gateway to the Grand Canyon, and only 146 miles (234 kilometres) from the almost snow-free desert city of Phoenix (it received a dusting in 1990), can accumulate more than 200 inches (508 centimetres) of snow in a season because it is 7,000 feet (2,130 metres) above sea level.

What was the world's coldest year?

In 1600, a 16,000-foot (4,850-metre) Peruvian mountain

erupted with great force. Called Huaynaputina, meaning "new volcano" in Quechua, an Incan language, the volcano spewed dust for hundreds of miles and mudflows travelled 75 miles (120 kilometres) to the Pacific Ocean. Ash made it into the stratosphere and spread across the northern hemisphere, helping to make 1601 the coldest year ever measured.

The next coldest year was also caused by a volcano. In 1815, Mount Tambora, a volcano in the seismically active Indonesian island chain, registered the largest eruption in more than 1,600 years and brought on 1816's year without a summer. The eruption was said to have killed 92,000 people near the volcano. An estimated 100,000 people died in Europe because the unseasonably cold weather killed crops, bringing on famine.

How much of the Mississippi River has ever frozen in wintertime?

In 1784, the Mississippi froze its full length, right past New Orleans, and ice made it to the Gulf of Mexico. Ice chunks reached New Orleans in 1899, though the freeze stopped at Cairo, Illinois, where the Ohio River joins the Mississippi and doubles its volume.

The long, cold winter of 1784 followed an eruption of the Laki volcano in Iceland in 1783.

Where is the world's coldest place?

The lowest temperature ever recorded in the world was -128.6°F (-89.2°C) at Vostok, Antarctica, in 1983. The Russian research station, located at the southern geomagnetic pole and near the Southern Pole of Inaccessibility — which is as far away from anywhere else as you can possibly get — has thirty inhabitants during the summer, and half that in the winter.

Vostok had its warmest summer day a year earlier, when temperatures soared to a bone-chilling -2.2°F (-19°C). Average winter temperatures hover in the -85°F (-65°C) range. In the summer they rise to -22°F (-30°C).

Vostok is colder than the South Pole, 600 miles (965 kilometres) away, because it is at a higher altitude — 11,220 feet (3,420 metres) instead of 9,000 feet (2,743 metres).

Where was the coldest temperature in Canada recorded?

A temperature so low it exceeded the range of the thermometers on hand was registered at Snag, Yukon, on February 3, 1947. That day the temperature fell to at least -81.4°F (-63°C).

Snag was established during the Second World War as a site for an emergency airstrip used when aircraft were being ferried to Siberia to help the Soviet Union in its war against Hitler's Germany. The base closed in 1968, but a Native settlement remains nearby.

Where is the "Pole of Cold"?

The Arctic is not all that cold. Temperatures at the North Pole average -24°F (-31°C) in the wintertime and get up to 32°F (0°C) during the summer. The real cold spot north of the equator is Russia's "Pole of Cold," south of the Arctic Circle in Siberia. Two towns in this area fight to be considered the world's coldest permanently inhabited communities. Verkhoyansk, population 1,500, has official recognition with a temperature of -93.6°F (-69.8°C). Oymyakon, a town of 800, created by the Soviet government to encourage nomadic reindeer herders in northern Siberia to modernize, claims a reading of -96.2°F (-71.2°C), using methods that did not meet official standards.

How do people deal with extreme cold?

Bitterly cold temperatures for half the year give Verkhoyansk and Oymyakon problems rarely faced anywhere else. For instance, diesel fuel freezes at -58°F (-50°C), and lubricating grease freezes as well, so engines that sit in extreme cold must be kept warm with fires and axle grease needs to be heated with blowtorches. If the power fails, pipes freeze within hours.

Where is the world's toughest dog sled race?

In temperatures that can be as cold as -58°F (-50°C), a race of at least 1,049 miles is run between Anchorage and Nome, Alaska. The Iditarod (the name comes from the Athabascan language) was held for the first time in 1973. Martyn Buser recorded the best time when he won the race in 8 days, 22 hours, 46 minutes, and 2 seconds in 2002.

Which pole has the most ice?

Ninety percent of the world's ice is locked up in the Antarctic ice sheet, which is about a mile thick in most places. Arctic ice is like a thin skin over the 13,000-foot (4,000-metre) deep Arctic Ocean. The Arctic ice cap is 6 to 10 feet (1.8 to 3 metres) thick, and half of it naturally melts or freezes with the seasons.

Lately, climatologists have been expressing concern that things are changing at both poles. In the Antarctic chunks of ice as big as the state of Rhode Island have recently broken away from the continent. In the Arctic, the ice cap is shrinking and getting thinner every year.

HEAT

Which American state would you think has the highest recorded temperature, Hawaii or Alaska?

If you thought Hawaii, you would be wrong. For almost sixteen years, starting in June 1915, Fort Yukon in Alaska held the record for the highest temperature in the two states, at 100°F (38°C). On April 27, 1931, Pahala, Hawaii, tied Fort Yukon, and the records still stand.

Where was Canada's highest temperature recorded?

On July 5, 1937, Yellow Grass and Midale, two towns in southern Saskatchewan, recorded temperatures of 114°F (46°C). This dry area of flat prairie endures severe temperature fluctuations. During the summer, the mercury often exceeds 100°F (38°C), plunging to -22°F (-30°C) in the winter months.

Where is the hottest place in the world?

El Azizia in Libya has held the record as the world's hottest place since 1922, when a temperature of 136°F (58°C) was recorded. Not surprisingly, Death Valley, California, registered the highest temperature ever recorded in North America at 134°F (57°C). Extreme as these temperatures are, they are recorded in the shade in an enclosure that is about 5 feet (1.5 metres) off the ground and open to whatever breeze may be present. Temperatures on the ground in the sun would be much hotter.

Which place holds the world record for the most consecutive days with temperatures of 100°F (38°C) or more?

Temperatures at Marble Bar, in northwest Australia, exceeded 100°F (38°C) for 162 consecutive days in 1923–24. Death Valley, California, had at least forty days with temperatures above 120°F (49°C) in 1996.

What is the highest Humidex reading ever recorded?

A Canadian invention from 1965, the Humidex aims to help us understand how heat and moisture in the air work together to make us feel hotter. It compares to the U.S. Heat Index, though it renders higher temperature equivalents. The highest Humidex reading ever recorded in Canada, was 126°F (52°C) in Windsor, Ontario.

How hot does it get at the North and South poles?

At the geographic North Pole, where your location can change because you are sitting on a floating ice sheet, surface summer temperatures, particularly in July, hover around the freezing mark or slightly above. At Amundsen-Scott South Pole Station the temperature has struggled up to 7°F (-14°C), still pretty darned cold.

Another North Pole, a town near Fairbanks, Alaska, enjoys 80°F (27°C) temperatures in the summer. Every year, millions of letters to Santa are sent there.

What was unsettling about the winter of 2006-07?

During the period from December 2006 to February 2007, worldwide temperatures were warmer than at any time since record keeping began. However, the effects were far from uniform. For instance, while North America experienced numerous hotspots in this period, it was cold or seasonal in other areas, so overall temperatures for the continent were about normal.

DROUGHT

What is the world's largest desert?

Antarctica has a desert that covers 5.3 million square miles (14 million square kilometres). In comparison, the world's largest non-polar desert is the Sahara at 3.5 million square miles (9 million square kilometres). A region qualifies as a desert if it receives less than ten inches (sixteen centimetres) of precipitation in a year. Deserts can be warm, cold, or temperate.

Where are you least likely to need a raincoat?

Sheltered from moist ocean air by a west coast mountain range and flanked by the Andes to the east, the world's

That the Sahara is at least three times bigger than its nearest non-polar rival? Some of the other great deserts include:

- Arabian in the Arabian Peninsula: 900,000 square miles (2.3 million square kilometres)
- Gobi in Mongolia-China: 500,000 square miles (2.3 million square kilometres)
- Patagonian in Argentina: 260,000 square miles (675,000 square kilometres)
- Great Victoria in Australia: 250,000 square miles (650,000 square kilometres)
- Kalahari in southern Africa: 225,000 square miles (580,000 square kilometres)
- Great Basin in Nevada, U.S.: 190,000 square miles (490,000 square kilometres)
- Great Sandy in Australia: 150,000 square miles (390,000 square kilometres)

driest desert sits on a plateau about 8,000 feet (2,400 metres) above sea level in the northern part of Chile. The Atacama is thought to have gone without rain for four hundred years at one stretch, from 1571 until 1971. Parts of it have been compared to Mars.

What is the Sahel?

This band of arid grassland stretches across Africa, on the southern fringe of the Sahara Desert, in so-called sub-Saharan Africa. It relies heavily on the African monsoons for six to twenty inches (fifteen to forty-five centimetres) of water annually, and suffers frequent, lengthy droughts when the monsoons do not come. In 1984, the eastern Sahel, gripped in drought, began to suffer famine as well. Reports of the famine reached the West, generating massive public support for a relief effort. Famously, pop stars led by Bob Geldof came together to produce a fundraising song called "We Are the World."

How does drought affect Canada?

Like the United States, Canada's Prairies suffered through the Dust Bowl of the dirty thirties and lesser events in the 1890s and early 1980s. In 2001–02, drought affected all of Canada again. The Prairies were hit particularly hard, especially in a number of areas that had already been putting up with several years of dry weather, and the Great Lakes registered record low lake levels. The cost of the drought in 2002 is estimated at $5 billion.

What is the longest period a mammal can go without drinking water?

The kangaroo rat gets its water from the seeds it eats and

Significant Droughts

- In 2005, the Amazon experienced its worst drought in a century. Suggested causes included deforestation and ocean warming induced by climate change.
- In 2003, dry weather and heat overwhelmed Europe and Great Britain. About 35,000 people are estimated to have died, almost 15,000 in France alone. Britain experienced its first day with temperatures above 100°F (38°C).
- In the 1930s, drought in the United States and the Canadian Prairies led to massive crop losses and farm foreclosures, and deepened the Depression started by the 1929 stock market crash. At its peak in 1934, the "Dust Bowl" stretched from New York to California.

by recycling its waste products, and it doesn't need to ever take a drink. Just as well, because it lives in Death Valley. Humans, on the other hand, would be lucky to last three days there without water.

Why are China's deserts growing?

In China's northwest desertification is taking place at an alarming rate. The pressure to feed 1.3 billion people is great. Consequently, China's government has encouraged intensive agricultural practices. That, combined with several years of drought, has turned the area into a dust bowl. Recently, dust from the region carried all the way across the Pacific Ocean, finally coming down in western North America, where it is a growing pollution issue.

Chinese cities like Beijing are regularly blanketed by this dust, as are parts of North and South Korea and Japan.

Why was Central Asia hit by an unusually severe drought near the millennium?

Countries along the route of the legendary Silk Road through Central Asia suffered through more than three years of drought from 1999 to 2002. Afghanistan and northern Iran were particularly hard hit, as were Uzbekistan and Tajikistan, two countries formed following the breakup of the Soviet Union. Climate change theory anticipates that droughts will become more frequent and longer in this region as it warms up, so this drought was not really a surprise. However, the drought also coincided with a prolonged La Niña, which has led to drier conditions in the area in the past, illustrating why natural climate variability makes it difficult to conclusively associate climate change with a specific weather event.

FLOODS

Where was the world's most disastrous flood?

Flooding on an almost unimaginable scale took place in July and August 1931, along China's Yangtze River. Almost 4 million people lost their lives in this disaster, and nearly 50 million were displaced. This flood and others helped provide justification for the huge and controversial Three Gorges Dam project, which has also displaced many people and possibly led to the extinction of the Yangtze River dolphin.

Why do floods cause so much death in Bangladesh?

Sandwiched between India and Myanmar (formerly

Burma), Bangladesh is a low-lying country on the coast of the Bay of Bengal. Disastrous floods are common there because huge storms are a feature of its monsoon season and much of the country is at sea level, but one that followed the Bhola cyclone on November 12–13, 1970, was almost too much to bear. Estimates of the death toll range from 200,000 to more than 500,000. The number of people displaced was estimated at 50 million, more than a third of the country's population. About 1 million cattle were also destroyed.

What happened after the Bhola cyclone?

In spite of the clear message sent by the 1970 storm and several of its predecessors, getting the country's poor out of flood-prone areas appears almost impossible. Another large cyclone struck on April 29–30, 1991, bringing death to another 150,000 people and displacing 10 million. Strategies now in place to reduce future death tolls include elevated shelters and an army of emergency workers.

What was North America's biggest flood?

Rainfall as much as two to three times normal during the first half of 1993 and heavy downpours that couldn't soak in to already saturated soil led to the Mississippi River and many of its tributaries, including the Missouri, being above flood stage for 144 days from April to the end of September. Over $20 billion worth of damage was done and fifty people lost their lives.

Who gets Canada's worst floods?

Manitoba's Red River Valley gets some sort of flood almost every spring, and in 1997 it got a doozy. The flooding was really North American as it started where the Red River separates Grand Forks, North Dakota, from Grand Forks, Minnesota. Those states experienced $2 billion in damage when flood waters overwhelmed 49-foot (15-metre) dikes and levies with 54-foot (16.5-metre) peak levels. In Canada, the river peaked at almost 22 feet (7 metres), but defences held in all but the town of St. Agathe, keeping the cost of the flood to about $800 million. For a time, however, the Red River was dubbed the "Red Sea" as it spread out to cover over 900 square miles (2,330 square kilometres).

Canada's costliest flood was in Quebec's Saguenay River Valley, from July 18 to 21, 1996. Damage was estimated at about $1 billion.

Which country has been keeping flood data for the longest time?

China has seven major rivers and experiences monsoons and other intense storms. Half of the country's population lives in flood-prone areas. Floods are important there, which is why accurate record keeping stretches back more than two thousand years.

RAIN

Where is the world's wettest place?

The Indian state of Meghalaya, meaning "home of the clouds" in Hindi, boasts the town of Cherrapunji, which was soaked by 905 inches (2,299 centimetres) of rain during a twelve-month period beginning in August 1860 and ending in July 1861. This town of about ten thousand people also holds the record for the wettest month. In July 1861, 366 inches (930 centimetres) of rain were measured, enough water to completely cover a two-storey house.

The nearby town of Mawslynram vies with Hawaii's Mt. Waialeale for an average annual rainfall record that exceeds 460 inches (1,168 centimetres). For seventy-four consecutive years, Cherrapunji experienced 450 inches (1,143 centimetres) per year.

The Kekaha coastal region is just fifteen miles (twenty-five kilometres) from Mt. Waialeale, but it sits in a rain shadow and gets only 20 inches (32 centimetres) of rain annually.

Why is Cherrapunji so wet?

Cherrapunji sits on the side of a mountain at an altitude of about 4,000 feet (1,200 metres). The Bay of Bengal, where summer monsoons form, is to the south. As the warm, moist air from the monsoons comes up against the mountainside, it gives up rain in great quantities.

In recent years, this pattern seems to be changing. Rainfall has dropped to about a third of historic levels, and the town is often forced to import water to meet its needs. Climate change and rapid deforestation are cited as possible culprits.

Henderson Lake on the southwest of Vancouver Island is the wettest place in Canada, with an average rainfall of 262 inches (665.5 centimetres).

Quickies

Did you know ...

- that most snow falls at a leisurely walking pace of 1 to 4 miles per hour (1.5 to 6 kilometres per hour), but winds can whip it into a frenzy?
- that drizzle jogs to earth at 6 to 10 miles per hour (10 to 15 kilometres per hour)?
- that rain gallops to the ground at 12 to 15 miles per hour (20 to 25 kilometres per hour)?
- that the heavy rain pelting you during a downpour bursts from the clouds at more than 20 miles per hour (30 kilometres per hour)?
- that big hailstones can hit you at speeds greater than 105 miles per hour (170 kilometres per hour), faster than the hardest pitch thrown by a major-league-baseball fastballer?

Where was the most rain ever recorded from a cyclone?

As big as Rhode Island, and a little more than half the size of Prince Edward Island, a small volcanic dot in the middle of the Indian Ocean called Reunion holds three world records for rain from a cyclone. During Tropical Cyclone Hyacinthe in January 1980, one part of the island was soaked by 223.5 inches (567.7 centimetres) of rain in ten days, while another received 127.6 inches (324.1 centimetres) in just seventy-two hours, and a third was drenched by 46 inches (117 centimetres) in just twelve hours. In 1966, it set a record for rain in a twenty-four-hour span of 72 inches (183 centimetres).

Reunion was uninhabited when the Portuguese discovered it in 1513. Today more than 750,000 people live there. It is governed by France.

What are monsoons?

Monsoons are rainy periods that regularly, though not always predictably, soak parts of every continent except Europe and Antarctica. There are monsoons in the summer and in the winter. Summer monsoons develop as cool ocean air is drawn onto very hot land, giving up moisture as it rises against obstacles like the Himalayas. The winter monsoons, triggered by air flowing from land to sea, are drier. Between monsoons, there is usually very little rain, making water storage a high priority. Cherrapunji got the vast majority of its world record rainfall during a three-month period.

Monsoon comes from the Arabic word *mausim*, which translates as "season."

Where was the most intense rainstorm ever measured?

It took just forty-two minutes for a storm to dump a foot of rain on the town of Holt, Missouri, on June 22, 1947. Its consequences were far-reaching even though only a small area was affected by the event. Local flooding followed the rainstorm, and the water poured into the Missouri River, which was already running high, contributing to record-breaking floods in St. Louis.

Quickies

Did you know ...
- that monsoons don't just occur in India and Africa — we have them here in North America, too? The North American or Mexican monsoon affects parts of Mexico and the American Southwest from June to September. Desert areas in the region get most of their precipitation from it.

Other Monsoon Systems
- Southwest (Indian Ocean) summer monsoon — mainly affects India (June to August)
- Northeast winter (retreating) monsoon — affects India and Australia (December to March)
- African (Sahelian) monsoons — affect equatorial Africa to 10° north (May to August)
- South American monsoon — affects Brazil and Bolivia (summer)

WIND

How are winds classified?

Although ways of classifying wind conditions had been around for centuries, the man whose system finally gained widespread acceptance was Sir Francis Beaufort, a British naval officer. He first used his scale in his personal journals in 1806, while commander of HMS *Woolwich*. The British Navy adopted the scale in 1838, following its use on HMS *Beagle*, the ship that took Charles Darwin on his epic journey to the Galapagos.

Beaufort's original scale helped a ship's captain set the appropriate amount of sail for the weather conditions. Over the next 150 years, it underwent many revisions. In 1906, a version for land, based on the behaviour of trees, was developed, and the nautical version was revised. Towards the end of the Second World War, a version that is still used in parts of Asia expanded the scale from the original 0 to 12 (dead calm to hurricane force) to 0 to 17. The numbers 13 to 17 describe conditions in a typhoon.

What's in a name?

Most people think of chinooks as warm prairie winds, but that is not how the name started out. Originally, a chinook wind was a moist wind blowing off the Pacific, so named by settlers because it seemed to come from the land of the Chinookian Indians. The name travelled to the prairies with French voyageurs.

Why are prairie chinooks warm?

The Pacific westerlies come ashore with lots of moisture and deposit huge quantities of rain and snow on Oregon, Washington, and British Columbia. When they come up against the Rockies they cool and the last bits of moisture are wrung out of them through condensation. Once they cross the Rocky Mountains, they descend to the American and Canadian plains. As the winds sweep down the mountain slopes, they warm up as much as 36°F (20°C) through compression of the air caused by increased pressure at lower altitudes.

What is the dark side of chinooks?

Chinooks happen all year round, and they can cause serious problems, especially in summer. They are moisture starved, so they quickly soak up any water they come across. They can turn a forest into a tinderbox and make a farmer's field an arid desert. They have been known to melt snow so fast that puddles do not even form, which is why some Native tribes called them "snow-eaters."

How did chinooks threaten the 1988 Calgary Olympics?

Normally Calgary, Alberta, is reliably cold during the winter months. However, the possibility of a chinook is always there. During the sixteen days of the Calgary Winter Olympics, chinooks behaved like impetuous sprites, wreaking all kinds of havoc. Temperatures bounced from −22˚F (-30°C) to 54˚F (12°C) overnight, and winds topped 70 miles per hour (112 kilometres per hour). In the end, organizers were forced to reschedule thirty-three events.

What is the mistral?

These cold, dry winds come down the slopes of the Alps and the Massif Central in France, picking up speed as they funnel through the Rhône valley, and continue on to the

Mediterranean. At one time, a defence of madness induced by the mistral was sometimes allowed to excuse crimes.

How do Santa Ana winds bring fires to Los Angeles?

The Santa Anas (Santanas) come into Los Angeles and San Diego, California, from the Great Basin between the Sierra Nevadas and the Rocky Mountains as hot, dry winds that can reach hurricane force. They dry out the chaparral scrub in the canyons and hills, creating ideal conditions for wildfires. The development of expensive homes on these hillsides has meant that in recent years the fires have caused millions of dollars in damage and taken many lives. A version of these winds that strikes San Francisco is called the diablo.

> **Quickies**
> *Did you know...*
> • that chinooks, Santa Anas, diablos, mistrals, boros, and foehn winds are all katabatic winds because they flow down mountainsides? *Katabatic* is from the Greek *katabatikos*, meaning "go down."

Where are the world's strongest katabatic winds?

The French Antarctic station of Dumont d'Urville, on Petral Island near the coast of Adélie Land in Antarctica has recorded katabatic wind gusts of 200 miles per hour (320 kilometres per hour).

What are valley breezes?

Valley breezes are the opposite of katabatic winds. Called anabatic winds, they happen when air is drawn up mountain slopes that have warmed in the sun. These winds are an important source of lift for gliders.

Where are foehn winds?

A foehn wind is a warm wind that blows down the north side of the Alps, towards Germany. They often raise avalanche fears because they warm and destabilize snow on the mountain slopes.

What is a haboob?

Haboobs are sand or dust storms that occur in the more arid regions of the Sahara (such as the Sudan) and in Texas and Arizona in the United States. The storms form at the end of thunderstorms. The fiercest examples move as fast as 50 miles per hour (80 kilometres per hour).

When was the jet stream discovered?

One of the most important, but least recognized, influences on North American climate is the jet stream. Until the end of the Second World War, no one even knew jet stream winds existed, although people who flew suspected something was going on. Jet streams are rivers of air that flow from west to east at altitudes of 20,000 to 50,000 feet (6,000 to 15,000 metres) and speeds of 30 to 400 miles per hour (48 to 640 kilometres per hour). Airline pilots jump onto them save fuel and shave time off west-to-east flights. The jet stream in North America forms where arctic air masses collide with warm air from the south. Its position is a good predictor of stormy weather.

Where are the world's strongest winds?

An observatory on the side of 6,288-foot (1,916-metre) Mount Washington in New Hampshire recorded a 231-mile-per-hour (370-kilometre-per-hour) wind gust on April 12, 1934, during a major storm that led to wind speeds unusual even for that windy location. In 1997, Typhoon Paka was reported to have had gusts of 236 miles per hour (380 kilometres per hour) when it made landfall on Guam, but the measuring device was later deemed unreliable.

SNOW

What is the world's snowiest place?

Snow depth is difficult to measure because snowdrifts melt and settle. The most reliable measurements are obtained by placing a white board on the ground next to a stake and measuring the snow that accumulates there. The Cascade mountain range in Washington State appears to be the world's snowiest place. Paradise, a small town on the southern slope of Mount Rainier, one of several active volcanoes in the Cascade range, had the twelve snowiest months ever recorded between February 19, 1971, and February 18, 1972, when 1,224.5 inches (3,110 centimetres) of snow was said to have fallen. Mount Baker, also in the Cascades and easily seen from Vancouver, British Columbia, had 1,140 inches (2,895 centimetres) in 1998–99. That is the record officially accepted by the United States National Weather Service.

Why do the Cascades get so much snow?

The same moist air off the Pacific that sustains the great rain forests of northern California, Oregon, Washington, and British Columbia is the reason these mountains are so snowy. As the moisture is forced up the mountainsides, it freezes at about 4,000 feet (1,200 metres) and falls as snow because the thinning air cannot hold it.

Where was the world's biggest one-day snowfall?

Silver Lake, Colorado, had almost 76 inches (193 centimetres) of snow on April 14 and 15, 1921. The Canadian record of 57 inches (145 centimetres) was set on February 11, 1999, at Tahtsa Lake in the Whitesail range of the Coast Mountains on the Nechako River, a major tributary of the Fraser River.

Where are you likely to find huge accumulations of drifting snow?

Mountain passes can pose huge challenges to railwaymen trying to keep freight moving in the wintertime. As if storms bringing snowfalls in excess of 100 inches (250 centimetres) are not bad enough, drifting can increase the depth of snow accumulated on the line to more than five times that much. When the Central Pacific Railroad was being constructed through the Sierra Nevadas, snowdrifts as deep as 60 feet (18 metres) had to be dealt with. Workers often blasted their way through, as if going through solid rock.

What is lake effect snow?

They do not set world records, but lake effect snowstorms can certainly deliver a punch. An unusually warm December 2006 and January 2007 stopped ice formation on Lake Ontario, then dry February winds crossed the open water picking up moisture. When the winds came ashore on the southeast end of the lake in Oswego County, New York, they dumped up to 141 inches (358 centimetres) of snow on the ground over a ten-day period. At one stage, the U.S. National Weather Service reported accumulations of as much as 5 inches (12.7 centimetres) an hour.

Where is the most snow at sea level?

Huge snowfalls generally happen at altitude, on mountainsides or plateaus. The port city of Valdez, Alaska, elevation zero, is an exception: it gets about 300 inches (762 centimetres) annually.

How much salt is used on Canadian roads?

The United States uses an estimated 10 million tons (9 million tonnes) of salt each year to melt ice on the roads. Europe uses about 4 million tons (3.6 million tonnes) a year. Canada comes in at about 5 million tons (4.5 million tonnes). These numbers fluctuate wildly depending upon the severity of the winter.

What is being done to make road salt better for the environment?

Road salt is thought to be toxic to many plants that grow alongside roadways and can make the water in wells near roadways unpalatable, but it is not thought to be dangerous to human health.

To reduce the amount of salt used, many strategies are being explored. One is pre-de-icing, which entails sending out the salt trucks before the storm hits. The idea is that salting in advance will prevent ice formation, reducing the total amount of salt that is required. Another strategy is better application control, and a third involves using instruments planted in the roadbed to provide advance warning of conditions that lead to icing.

HAIL

Why do hailstones have rings?

Like tree rings, hailstone rings are growth records. Hailstones form in a cloud as they are tossed from higher to lower to higher altitudes by updrafts and downdrafts until they become too heavy and fall to the ground. As they move through the cloud, water droplets freeze on them either quickly, catching air bubbles and giving them a milky ring, or slowly, forming a clear ring.

What is the largest hailstone ever measured?

In 2003, a hailstone found in Aurora, Nebraska, measured 7 inches (17.8 centimetres) across and 18.75 inches (47.6

centimetres) around its widest point, weighed in at 1.7 pounds (0.8 kilograms). In Bangladesh, a hailstone found in 1986 officially weighed in at 2.25 pounds (1 kilogram), but was not measured. Unofficially, an 11-pound (5-kilogram) hailstone was claimed in China in 1986.

How dangerous are hailstones?

Hailstones have killed people, sometimes in great numbers. On April 14, 1986, ninety-two people died in the Gopalganj district of Bangladesh following a hailstorm with stones weighing more than a kilogram. Hailstorms in North America have taken human life occasionally, but never in such horrific numbers. Animals have also suffered grievously. In one storm in Montana, more than two hundred sheep are said to have died. A storm in southern Alberta took the lives of more than 36,000 ducks in 1953.

What are the property losses from hailstorms?

Storm chasers in the southwestern United States, in the area known as Tornado Alley, frequently have their vehicles dented and even wrecked by hail. When big hailstones hit big cities like St. Louis, Dallas, and Denver, insured losses can exceed $1 billion. Routinely, hailstorms cause crop losses in the millions of dollars and end many dreams of a comfortable retirement.

Where is the hailiest place in the world?

A region shared by India, Bangladesh, and Nepal gets 10 to 13 days a year. Second-place Kenya, in eastern Africa, averages 10 or 11 hail days a year, but boasts the hailiest town. Kericho, notable for tea plantations, endures hail an average of 132 days a year.

FOG

Where is the world's foggiest place?

Cape Race, Newfoundland, experiences more than 158 fog days each year, more than any place else in the world. London, England, historically well known for pea soup fogs caused by pollution from coal furnaces, remains foggy today, but with only thirty days per year does not set any records.

What happened in London, England, between December 5 and December 9, 1952?

Cold weather and a mixture of sulphur dioxide, nitrogen oxide, and other pollutants from coal and industry combined to create a sooty, dirty, yellow-green fog. Called the "Great Smog," it is thought to have killed or contributed to the deaths of up to 16,000 people.

Disasters Influenced by Fog ...

- September 3, 1999: A 145-vehicle pileup killed 8 people and injured 150 on Highway 401 near Windsor, Ontario, when fog from Lake St. Clair suddenly reduced visibility.
- March 20, 1995: A 193-vehicle pileup on the Mobile Bay highway in Mobile, Alabama, killed one and sent ninety-one others to hospital.
- March 27, 1977: In fog, KLM Flight 4805 sliced away some of the fuselage and tail from Pan Am Flight 1736 during takeoff from Tenerife, one of the Canary Islands. Five hundred and eighty-three people were killed on the two flights. Miraculously, sixty-one of the Pan Am passengers survived. The planes were among several diverted from the main island because of a terrorist attack.
- April 20, 1914: The ocean liner *Empress of Ireland* collided with the coal carrier *Störstad* in the St. Lawrence River, north of Quebec City, and 1,167 lives were lost.

How are cloud forests formed?

The unusual environment created by Costa Rica's Monteverde Cloud Forest, and others like it, provides a home for plants and animals found nowhere else. Warm trade winds, full of moisture from the Caribbean Sea, cool as they go up the slopes of the Tilarán mountains. At about 4,000 feet (1,200 metres), where the forests are, moisture from the winds is surrendered as heavy mist and water droplets, which many plants, including hundreds of varieties of orchids, rely on in place of groundwater.

Why are climate scientists watching cloud forests?

In recent years, the mists of cloud forests have been thinning or moving up the mountains, leaving the forests dry.
Some amphibians have disappeared, and bird ranges are
changing. Many blame deforestation and ocean warming.

Twenty years ago, the golden tree frog disappeared
from Monteverde, an event that climate watchers point to
as the first extinction attributable to global warming.

STORMS

What is the lowest air pressure ever recorded during a storm?

At its most intense, a 1979 tropical storm called Super Typhoon Tip became a Category 5 cyclone with a sea level barometric pressure reading of 870 millibars, or 25.7 inches (65.3 centimetres) of mercury. A normal reading at sea level is 1013.2 millibars, or 29.92 inches (75.9 centimetres). The scale on most aneroid barometers does not go much below 28 inches (71.1 centimetres).

What are derechos?

A physics professor named Dr. Gustavus Hinrichs coined the word from Spanish in 1888 to describe powerful storms that featured straight-line winds, rather than the turning winds associated with tornadoes. Derechos are lines or bands of fast-moving thunderstorms that pack winds over 100 miles per hour (160 kilometres per hour). On July 4 and 5, 1999, a derecho moved from Ontario through southern Quebec to Maine, pulling up trees, damaging houses, and killing one person.

What is a nor'easter?

Nor'easters are born when a low-pressure system in the Gulf Stream collides with a high-pressure system from the Arctic. The storm is named for the northeasterly winds of the Arctic system, which force the storm up the coast of the United States and Canada until it heads off into the North Atlantic.

A nor'easter off the Grand Banks took 249 fishermen from Gloucester, Massachusetts, to their graves in 1879.

In 2006, a nor'easter brought 26.9 inches (68.3 centimetres) of snow to New York City's Central Park, more than ever before recorded there. Another storm in 1979 shut down Washington, D.C., while the Blizzard of '93 caused more than $1 billion in damage across North America.

What are "blue northers"?

Blue northers — the name originated among Texas cowboys — develop when a cold arctic air mass is pushed south quickly by the jet stream. These fast-moving storms are notable for blue-black clouds, rapid temperature drops of more than 50°F (28°C), and the cold, deep blue skies they leave behind. They can bring blizzards, but often do not. They frequently catch people and livestock in the open, where they freeze to death.

These systems are also called blue darters, blue whistlers, and Texas northers.

Where was the "Storm of the Century"?

At its height, this nor'easter, also called the Blizzard of '93, stretched from Nova Scotia to Central America. It brought unseasonably cold weather, snow that accumulated to depths of up to 5 feet (1.5 metres), thunderstorms, and a serial derecho that contained supercell thunderstorms, which spawned ten tornadoes in Florida.

Another storm was called the "Storm of the Century" before this one. That was the 1935 Labor Day hurricane. It hit the Florida Keys and would have caused little damage except that a large number of First World War veterans had been put to work there building a highway. They and their relatives were caught by the storm, and hundreds were killed while boarding the train sent to evacuate them.

Where was the world's greatest storm surge?

When powerful winds, such as those in a hurricane, blow towards shore, they can generate huge waves called storm surges. In 1899, the Mahina cyclone crossed Australia's Great Barrier Reef and entered Bathurst Bay, pushing a wall of water forty-three feet (thirteen metres) high.

During the November 12–13, 1970, Bhola cyclone in Bangladesh, unverified reports of storm surges as high as forty-nine feet (fifteen metres) were received.

A thirty-foot (nine-metre) storm surge overwhelmed the defences of New Orleans during Hurricane Katrina in 2005.

The Saffir-Simpson scale, which categorizes hurricane intensity on a scale of one to five, rates storms with a surge over eighteen feet (five and a half metres) as catastrophic.

What made Sebastian Junger's *Perfect Storm* perfect?

When a nor'easter off the southeast coast of Nova Scotia coast jostled with a low pressure system running along the U.S.-Canadian border and then combined with the considerable energy still present in a dying hurricane called Grace, conditions for a perfect storm were born. Around Halloween 1991, the huge system packed 60-mile-per-hour (100-kilometre-per-hour) winds and peak waves of 39 feet (11.8 metres). Some witnesses claimed some waves were as high as 100 feet (30.5 metres), and one of those is thought to have sunk a swordfish boat called the *Andrea Gail*, with six men on board. The boat and its fate became the focal point of Junger's book and the movie that followed.

How could the loss of the *Andrea Gail* have been averted?

The *Andrea Gail* carried an EPIRB (Emergency Position-Indicating Radio Beacon), which, had its signal been received, might have led rescuers to the boat and saved the lives of the crew. In a sad postscript to the tragedy, the Canadian Coast Guard found the device on Sable Island off the coast of Nova Scotia and quickly discovered why there was no signal: it was not turned on.

Weather forecasters learned a lot about storms from this experience. Storm warnings are now issued as much as four days in advance, giving ships like the *Andrea Gail* a reasonable amount of time to get out of the way.

Why do thunderstorms mostly occur in the late afternoon?

As the day unfolds, the sun warms the ground, encouraging evaporation that provides fuel for a storm at the end of the day. If warm low-level winds are also present, the storm may carry on into the evening. The orange hue that often accompanies thunderstorms is caused by the same atmospheric conditions that bring us beautiful sunsets.

Who has survived falling through a thunderstorm?

At least two people have fallen through thunderstorms and lived to talk about it. Probably the most famous is Lt. Col. William H. Rankin, a Marine Corps pilot whose jet suffered a malfunction, forcing him to eject. For forty-five minutes, he was supported in the thunderstorm by updrafts, and carried several thousand feet higher than when he had bailed out, before he was finally able to float safely to earth.

In January 2007, Ewa Wisnierska, a paraglider, was carried from 2,500 feet (760 metres) to over 32,000 feet (10,000 metres). She did not regain consciousness until she reached 1,600 feet (500 metres), which fortunately left her enough time to land. Another paraglider, caught in the same storm, was not so lucky.

Why do thunderclouds have an anvil shape?

The cumulonimbus clouds that bring thunderstorms build to great altitudes of as much as 70,000 feet (21,000 metres). There they encounter jet stream winds that slash through their tops, flattening them and stretching them out.

What makes supercells so dangerous?

Most violent tornadoes are spawned from supercells. These massive storms are also a source of large hail, flash flood–causing rains, and powerful lightning. Huge and slow moving, supercells can persist for hours in one location, causing a great deal of damage.

How bad is freezing rain?

From January 5 to 10, 1998, freezing drizzle fell on southern Quebec, central Ontario, New York, and Maine. Ice built up to more than 3 inches (7.5 centimetres) in some places. The weight of the ice pulled down tens of thousands of utility poles and countless trees, as well as 130 giant high-voltage transmission towers. Over 1.6 million people lost power, often for days.

A factor in the development of this unusual storm was an extremely strong El Niño (climate change, perhaps?) in 1997 and 1998, which influenced the course of the jet stream so it moved through the southern United States picking up moisture and then turned north to deposit it in the northern U.S. and Canada.

Damage in Canada due to the storm totalled about $4.2 billion. In Maine, the total was $340 million.

Where was the world's strongest cyclone?

Cyclone Monica formed on the Coral Sea off the northeast tip of Australia. On April 19, 2006, it crossed the Cape York Peninsula and intensified to Category 5 status in the Gulf of Carpentaria. A barometric pressure reading of 905 millibars was obtained on April 23 as it tracked slightly north of Australia's coast. Wind gusts reached 215 miles per hour (350 kilometres per hour). Although intense, Monica was a small cyclone, just 60 miles (95 kilometres) across. Fortunately, it passed through lightly populated areas, causing little damage and no deaths.

Other Major Freezing Rain Events ...

- December 9, 2002: Ice and 100–mile-per-hour (160-kilometre-per-hour) winds sank a patrol boat and exploration vessel in Novorosisk, a port in southern Russia on the Black Sea.
- November 6–13, 1969: Thirty transmission towers being constructed to bring power to Quebec City from power dams on the Manicouagan River were toppled in a huge ice storm.
- October 11, 1967: Freezing rain fell for eleven hours at Schefferville, Quebec.
- January 1–3, 1961: An ice storm in northern Idaho deposited as much as eight inches (twenty centimetres) of ice.

HURRICANES

How does the Saffir-Simpson hurricane scale work?

For a tropical storm to get on this scale and be considered a Category 1 hurricane, maximum winds must exceed 74 miles per hour (119 kilometres per hour). Such a storm will likely do superficial damage to trees and create storm surges that are 4 to 5 feet (1.2 to 1.5 metres) high. Category 5 hurricanes at the top end of the scale will generate winds of more than 155 miles per hour (249 kilometres per hour) and storm surges of 18 feet (5.5 metres) or more. If these storms, or even the much weaker Category 3s and Category 4s, hit populated areas, damage will be extensive to catastrophic. For example, Hurricane Katrina was only Category 3 when it came ashore, and look what it did.

What is the most hurricanes ever recorded in a single year?

In the 2005 Atlantic hurricane season, twenty-seven named storms were tracked, fifteen of which were hurricanes, three more than the previous record. Four of the hurricanes reached Category 5 status, two more than ever before — and all four caused a great deal of destruction. They were Emily, Katrina, Rita, and Wilma. The last three all struck parts of the United States. Emily confined its damage to Grenada, the Yucatan Peninsula, and Mexico.

The fewest hurricanes recorded in a single year was one, in 1890.

What's the most damage ever done by a hurricane?

Hurricane Katrina in 2005 will probably be the most expensive hurricane in history, with damage, insured and uninsured, thought to exceed $125 billion. But even hurricanes that don't make landfall are expensive. Hurricane warnings, typically issued when the storm is still 300 miles (480 kilometres) off the coast, cost an estimated $50 million for work interruptions and storm-proofing of buildings, even if the storm misses. Naturally, many people are trying to reduce the need for both types of expenditures by tracking storms more accurately.

Why was Hurricane Katrina so destructive?

Katrina struck the large city of New Orleans and overwhelmed its defences. First, it roared past a natural barrier of wetlands, already largely destroyed by human interference. Second, the so-called Barrier Islands were easily overcome by the storm surge. Third, the surge also breached and weakened levees, leaving the city to fill up with water like a cereal bowl (because much of it is below sea level).

New Orleans had not faced the full brunt of a major hurricane since Betsy in 1965. Before the disaster, critics felt the city's defensive preparations were inadequate to meet a challenge that was already overdue.

How many Category 5 hurricanes have hit the United States?

Before Hurricane Katrina, a Category 5 hurricane that came ashore as a Category 3, the most expensive hurricane in American history was a Category 5 storm called Andrew in 1993 that hit Miami, Florida, and cost $26.5 billion. It is one of only three hurricanes that were still Category 5 when they made landfall. The others were Camille in 1969 and the Labor Day hurricane that struck the Florida Keys in 1935, before hurricanes were given names.

Which was the deadliest hurricane on record?

Hurricane Mitch ranks as the deadliest in the past two centuries. It formed in the Caribbean in October 1998 and slowly moved through Central America, causing widespread flooding and up to 11,000 deaths before reaching Florida as a tropical storm. In 1900, Galveston, Texas, was struck by a Category 4 hurricane that swept over parts of the city that had been, in an act of hubris, built on a barrier island; it killed 8,000 people. A hurricane in 1780 is considered the most devastating of all, killing an estimated 22,000 people and decimating the Caribbean navies of Britain, France, and several other European countries during the American Revolution.

What was the most damaging hurricane to Canada?

Between October 15 and 17, 1954, Toronto, Ontario, suffered through the powerful last blasts of Hurricane Hazel. The storm had already caused devastation and death in Haiti, where up to a thousand people died, and in the United States, where one hundred lives were lost. In Toronto, it killed another eighty-three people and caused damage and flooding never seen in the city before or since.

What was the strongest hurricane to hit Canada?

Newfoundland's Avalon Peninsula received the brunt of a Category 3 hurricane called Luis in September 1995. The ocean liner *Queen Elizabeth 2* was in the area at the time, and it reported waves up to 100 feet (30 metres) high, as did a Canadian Nomad data collection buoy. The only other tropical storm to be rated as a hurricane when it made landfall in Canada hit Nova Scotia, south of Halifax, in 1893.

How often do hurricanes hit Canada?

About 40 percent of the tropical storms, including hurricanes, that form in the Atlantic each year make it to Canada. However, the trip north almost always saps their strength, reducing them to tropical storms or depressions by the time they cross the border. Over the past decade or so, an average of five storms made the journey each year. This compares to a hundred-year average of 3.3 storms, and reflects the increase in the number of storms being generated each year. Many scientists point to this increase as further proof of climate change due to warming oceans.

How often has Brazil been hit by hurricanes?

Could it be climate change? Up until March 2004, the South Atlantic was considered a hurricane-free zone because the ocean was too cold to sustain such large storms. Then Catarina came ashore in Brazil, in the province of the same name, leaving 38 people dead and 2,000 homeless.

Catarina was a Category 1 hurricane with winds of about 85 miles per hour (140 kilometres per hour).

Where do hurricanes form?

Hurricanes need water temperatures of about 80°F (27°C) to develop. The hurricanes that affect eastern North America usually form in the eastern Atlantic, in tropical latitudes, north of the equator. Hurricanes also form north and south of the equator in the Pacific, affecting Australia and parts of Asia, and south of the equator in the Indian Ocean, affecting Africa. Mexico's west coast also gets hit by Pacific hurricanes. A tropical storm becomes a hurricane when its winds exceed 74 miles per hour (119 kilometres per hour).

Where are hurricane winds most dangerous?

The right side of a hurricane is expected to be the most dangerous part of the storm. There the hurricane winds combine with steering winds, increasing the storm's intensity. The strongest and most unpredictable winds are in the eyewall, the ring of dark clouds surrounding the eye, where speeds can top 200 miles per hour (320 kilometres per hour).

TORNADOES

How does the Fujita tornado scale work?

The smallest tornado, Category 0, called an F0 on the scale, needs a wind of at least 40 miles per hour (64 kilometres per hour); otherwise, it will be considered a dust devil, whirlwind, sand auger, etc. Tornadoes of this intensity are likely to knock down a few trees and do minor property damage. At the other end of the scale, F5 storms can pack winds of 318 miles per hour (512 kilometres per hour), stronger than anything else seen at ground level. F5 tornadoes can carry houses and cars for hundreds of feet.

Where was Canada's worst tornado?

On June 30, 1912, Regina, Saskatchewan, faced a tornado that left twenty-eight dead and hundreds injured. The worst tornado in recent memory struck Edmonton, Alberta, on July 31, 1987. It cut a swath through parts of the city and through Strathcona County that was 25 miles (40 kilometres) long and up to 0.5 miles (0.8 kilometres) wide. The storm killed 27 people and injured 253. Rain and hail the size of softballs caused flooding and further damage.

Another well-remembered tornado event struck Barrie, Ontario, on May 31, 1985. That day, tornadoes took 8 lives, injured 155, and caused over $100 million in damage.

How do tornadoes form?

Although we send people to the moon and robots to Mars, tornadoes still have mysteries. What we do know is that they develop in several ways. The strongest occur when horizontal winds from several directions are drawn into the rotating updrafts of supercell thunderstorms. North of the equator, tornadoes rotate in a counter-clockwise direction. In the southern hemisphere the rotation is clockwise. On the rare occasions that tornadoes rotate in the opposite direction, they are called anti-cyclones.

Where are you most likely to get a tornado?

Tornadoes happen all over the world, but are most common in the United States. Surprisingly, Britain gets the most tornadoes per square mile. In 2004, the United States experienced a record 1,819 tornadoes. Canada gets about eighty twisters each year.

Which country suffers the most from tornadoes?

In terms of lives lost, Bangladesh has suffered the most. One storm in 1989 cost 1,300 lives, injured 12,000, and left tens of thousands homeless. Another in May 1996 killed more than 1,000, injured 34,000, and put 100,000 out of their homes.

In North America, a tornado touched down for 219 miles in Missouri, Illinois, and Indiana, taking the lives of 695 people and injuring more than 2,000. The last tornadoes to take more than a hundred lives in North America were in 1953 in Flint, Michigan, and Waco, Texas.

The costliest tornado ever was a Category 5 monster that struck Oklahoma City and a number of other Oklahoma towns in May 1999, causing over $1 billion in damage.

What is the connection between waterspouts and tornadoes?

Most waterspouts are tornadoes on water. While they are usually weak, they have been known to sink ships. Not long ago, in September 1970, a steam yacht was lost in the Gulf of Venice, near Italy, along with thirty-six passengers. Four centuries earlier, in the 1550s, ships in harbour on the island of Malta were destroyed and six hundred people died. In both these instances, the waterspouts later came ashore as tornadoes or landspouts and took more lives.

Waterspouts have also been accused of contributing to the Tay Bridge collapse in Britain in December 1879. Claims have been made that two or three were sighted during a howling gale near the two-mile-long bridge shortly before a train reached the middle and fell into the river with a loss of seventy-five passengers.

What is the most tornadoes in a single storm system?

The "Super Tornado Outbreak" of April 3–4, 1974, consisted of 148 tornadoes. Six were Category 5, and twenty-four were Category 4, the most ever. The toll was 330 people killed and more than 5,000 injured in eleven American states and in Windsor, Ontario.

Where was the world's highest tornado?

Rockwell Pass in California's Sequoia National Park was hit by a tornado that touched down at 12,000 feet (3,660 metres) on July 7, 2004. Tornadoes have also been observed crossing the Teton Range at 11,000 feet (3,350 metres).

Where was a luminous tornado photographed?

Only one photograph has ever been accepted as a genuine image of a luminous tornado. That was taken of a Category 4 tornado that swept through Toledo, Ohio, killing sixteen people, on April 11, 1965.

Quickies

Did you know ...

- that during 2003 and 2004, Oklahoma, in the heart of America's Tornado Alley, went a record 292 days without a tornado?
- that on one day, October 4, 1998, Oklahoma had twenty-seven tornados touch down?
- that six months after Hurricane Katrina, on February 2, 2006, two tornadoes struck New Orleans?
- that on April 5, 1936, an F5 tornado killed 233 people in Tupelo, Mississippi, but spared a very young Elvis Presley?
- that balls of fire preceded a 1971 tornado in Wray, Colorado?
- that in 2006, Idaho got only its second October tornado?

Wizard of Oz, anyone?

In 2006, two events, four days and half a world apart, showed that it is possible to be swept up by a tornado and live to tell the tale. On March 8 in South Canterbury, New Zealand, a tornado picked up a pig and dropped it into another pen, and on March 12 in Fordland, Missouri, a teenager was pulled out of his grandmother's mobile home and thrown more than 1,300 feet (400 metres).

What is the longest period that the United States has gone without a tornado?

Between December 12, 1985, and February 1, 1986, the country enjoyed a record fifty-two tornado-free days.

Where was the world's biggest waterspout?

Quickies

Did you know ...
- that tornadoes are also called twisters, ropes, funnel clouds (before they touch the ground), whirlwinds, wedges, windhoses, or cyclones? Smaller cyclonic events include dust devils, gustnados, and willy-willies.

A mining engineer equipped with a surveyor's theodolite was present when a cumulonimbus cloud produced a series of huge waterspouts off the coast of New South Wales, Australia, in 1898. He calculated that the second one was 5,014 feet (1,528 metres) high. In 1919, a sextant was used to measure a waterspout from the deck of the SS *War Hermit* near Cape Comorin, India. That waterspout was 4,600 feet (1,402 metres) high, as was another seen from the SS *Dallas Star* in 1950.

Have people survived being hit by a waterspout?

Waterspouts are often weak. A man who sailed through one said the winds inside were not more than thirty knots. In 1949, a pilot flew through a 1,200-foot (370-metre) waterspout at about 600 feet (180 metres) and only got his plane wet.

LIGHTNING

Where are you most likely to get hit by lightning?

Kifuka, a village in the Democratic Republic of the Congo in Central Africa, gets more lightning than anywhere else in the world (Uganda gets the most thunderstorms), according to imagery from NASA satellites. The North and South Poles almost never get lightning, and it is rare in the open ocean.

Florida gets the most lightning in North America. In Canada, lightning is most common near the U.S. border where Manitoba and Saskatchewan meet, in the foothills of the Rockies near Edmonton, Alberta, and in southwestern Ontario.

Who is at the greatest risk are from lightning?

Men are struck by lightning five times as often as women are, and it is not just because more men than women play golf (in the United States, only 5 percent of fatalities from lightning strikes are linked to golf). The people most likely to be struck by lightning are those enjoying other outdoor pursuits like hiking and camping. The people in greatest danger inside a house are those who try to use a landline phone.

Where is the most dangerous place to be in a thunderstorm?

If you are in a boat on open water, under an isolated tree or a large tree in a forest, or in the middle of a large open area like a golf course or soccer field, you are a prime candidate to be struck by lightning or injured by a falling tree. Should you feel your hair stand on end, get a tingling sensation on your skin, or hear a crackling sound, a lightning strike may be imminent. Your best bet then is to squat and make yourself into a ball in the hopes that the lightning will go around you and not damage internal organs.

Are planes in danger from lightning?

Two major crashes, and many smaller ones, especially in the early days of flight, have been attributed to lightning strikes. In 1971, a plane bound for Lima, Peru, flew into a thunderstorm. Lightning struck the right wing, setting it on fire, and the plane fell into the jungle. Ninety-two people were on board, and ninety-one died, seventy-seven in the crash and fourteen before they could be rescued. The lone survivor hiked along a stream for ten days until she reached a logging camp. Another crash in 1983 killed all eighty-one passengers and crew.

Nowadays, aircraft try to give thunderstorms a wide berth because their behaviour is just too unpredictable.

How many people die from lightning strikes?

In Canada, six to ten people die every year. In recent years, the United States has suffered an average of sixty-seven fatalities annually. Florida is the most lightning-prone area in the United States. Over a thirty-five-year period from 1959 to 1994, when 3,329 Americans died from lightning, the National Weather Service noted 350 deaths in that state, more than 10 percent of the total, and far more than North Carolina, which was second with 160 deaths.

Why is lightning so common in Florida?

The state is a long peninsula separating the Atlantic Ocean from the Gulf of Mexico. East winds blow inland from the Atlantic and west winds blow in from the Gulf, forcing the warm air of the state's interior upward to create thunderstorms and strong updrafts that provide conditions ideal for lightning formation.

Who survived the most lightning strikes?

A one-time park ranger in Virginia named Roy C. Sullivan endured seven lightning strikes. After the first four, he began to believe something was out to get him. The fifth time he was struck while trying to outrun a cloud that seemed to be chasing him. He was hit for the seventh time in 1977. He died tragically in 1983 when, at age seventy-one, he took his own life.

Quickies

Did you know ...

• that tall structures are designed to absorb frequent lightning strikes? Toronto's CN Tower gets clobbered a whopping seventy-five times a year.

• that most people are hit by lightning in the thirty minutes before or thirty minutes after a thunderstorm?

• that lightning bolts strike the Earth more than 3 billion times annually? Eighty-five percent of those strikes are on land.

• that lightning starts about 45 percent of Canadian forest fires and burns more than 80 percent of the timber lost?

What are the different types of lightning?

Lightning can occur between clouds, inside clouds, and from clouds to ground. The most common type is forked lightning, which we call sheet lightning when it is far away and the forks become indistinguishable from each other. Ball lightning is seen as a ball of light that moves slowly and sometimes ends with an explosion. Satellites, space shuttles, and high-flying aircraft have observed two other types of lightning on top of thunderheads: red sprites are weak discharges that shoot up above the cloud, and blue jets are cone-like emissions that travel up from the core of the thunderstorm to altitudes of twenty-five or thirty miles (forty or fifty kilometres).

The light we see from lightning occurs after it strikes the ground and is on its way back up to the cloud. The heat generated during the electrical discharge causes it.

BEAUTY

How do multiple rainbows happen?

You cannot touch a rainbow. They are optical phenomena that depend upon lighting conditions, moisture in the air, and the position of the viewer. Multiple rainbows are likely to be found at the foot of a waterfall. When fine mist is being thrown into the air and the sun is bright enough to create a strong primary rainbow, reflections off the water droplets create a mirror image of the original rainbow, which in turn creates a mirror image of itself, and so on until they become too faint to see.

What is a fire rainbow?

Fire rainbows are not true rainbows. On rare occasions they appear on wispy cirrus clouds at high altitudes. The clouds must be made up of hexagonal ice crystals that are parallel to the ground and bathed in light from a sun that is at least 58° above the horizon.

What are rainbow spokes?

Sometimes a rainbow looks like part of a wagon wheel with one or more spokes. The scattering of sunlight within the rainbow arc causes these spokes.

Can rainbows happen at night?

Lunar rainbows, known as moonbows, can and do happen if the moon is bright enough and no more than 42° above the horizon. Rain or a waterfall must be opposite to the moon for the moonbow to form.

They are sometimes called white rainbows, because colour is very rarely seen.

When do you get fogbows?

Fogbows appear in the fog, which is not surprising because they would be rainbows if the fog were replaced by rain. The secret to a fogbow is the minute size of the water droplets. The light is diffused, and it appears white because only pale yellow, white, and pale violet colours are emitted.

When do green rays appear?

Green rays are a magic moment in a sunset over the water. As the sun sinks below the horizon, it shines brightly red, and then, at last moment, just before it disappears altogether, an observer may catch a sudden flash of brilliant green.

When will you see a Brocken spectre?

This ghostly apparition got its name from a mountain in Germany, where it is seen frequently. Climbers are often surprised by them when they top a ridge and look down. Brocken spectres look like the indistinct images of large men, but they are actually the shadows of the climbers themselves. They are created by sunlight shining behind the climbers and projecting their shadows on the clouds, mist, or fog below.

How do sundogs form?

The sun's dogs, as northern people call them, are the mock suns that sometimes appear to the right and left of the sun, often along with a halo. Perfect sundogs form when sunlight shines through flat, hexagonal ice crystals and is bent 22°. When the angles are not optimal or some of the crystals are misshapen, colourful variations can occur.

What is a Fata Morgana?

A Fata Morgana (the name comes from the Italian for "Morgan le Fay," magical sister of King Arthur) is a superior mirage, the kind that appears above the object that it represents. These phenomena are formed when light is bent while moving through layers of cold and warm air. This mirage is the type that inspires notions of fairy castles in the air. They are common in the Arctic and in the Antarctic, as well as in parts of the Mediterranean.

An inferior mirage is seen below the object it is representing. We often see these mirages as shimmering puddles on the highway on hot days.

Why do auroras form at the poles?

Aristotle was awestruck by auroral displays. Pierre Gassendi, a seventeenth-century French chemist, called them auroras after the Greek goddess of dawn. These shimmering, glimmering curtains of light occur because the Earth's magnetic field captures charged particles from the sun — the solar wind — and channels them to the North and South Poles, where they collide with the gases that make up our atmosphere, producing a wonderful display of colours.

While auroras may appear to be close to us, they actually form at altitudes of sixty miles (ninety-five kilometres) or more in the thin air of the ionosphere.

The northern aurora, the Northern Lights, is the Aurora Borealis; the southern version is Aurora Australis.

CLIMATE CHANGE

What is the difference between climate change and global warming?

Global warming is a trigger for climate change. As the Earth's average temperature rises, weather, as we know it, is changing. For instance, the Arctic is warmer and pack ice is melting. Winter comes later and spring comes earlier. Storms are stronger and longer.

Scientists agree that the world is warming and human activity is contributing. They disagree on how much the climate will change as a result and what, if anything, we can or should do about it.

What are climate models?

Predicting weather is an extremely complex task, especially when we attempt to do it over many years over a vast area, as climate scientists are trying to do when they paint pictures of the world after global warming. Climate

Quickies

Did you know ...

- that global warming is extreme weather at a snail's pace?
- that all the years since 1998 have had temperatures well above historical averages?
- that at Sand Point in Alaska's Aleutian chain of islands, a very rare tornado was sighted on July 25, 2005?
- that at Banks Island in Canada's North, Inuit report thunder and lightning, rarely mentioned in their oral tradition?
- that Lake Chad in Africa has shrunk from about 10,000 square miles (16,000 square kilometres) to just 500 square miles (800 square kilometres) since 1963?
- that many glaciers are retreating and ice caps on some mountaintops are disappearing?
- that permafrost is thawing, forcing some northern communities to relocate?
- that sea levels are rising because warmer oceans take up more space?
- that 2005 was a record hurricane season for both the power and number of storms?
- that since 1970, the Arctic Oscillation has spent more time in a positive mode, which means warmer, shorter winters in temperate areas?
- that the Gulf Stream has slowed down 30 percent in recent years?

models are the tool they use. These computer programs are tested against known weather phenomena, then put to work forecasting the future. Scientists adjust them continually, as they learn more about climate and computers become more powerful.

What makes it difficult to communicate the climate change argument?

The main difficulty is it is not just one storm. Climate change is all sorts of events happening over a long period a little bit differently from the way they did before. For instance, while rainfall has remained relatively constant across the United States over the past ninety years, heavy downpours are 20 percent more frequent. This translates into more flooding and erosion and less benefit for plants, animals, and water reservoirs. Trends like this are being noticed all over the world, a little bit here and a little bit there — not enough to make the front pages, but enough that in time we may all feel mighty uncomfortable.

What is anthropogenic forcing?

Anthropogenic is a term that gets thrown around a lot these days when talking about climate change and global warming. It means that humans did it. A *forcing*, in meteorological terms, is an external influence on climate. The carbon dioxide we release when we drive a car or generate electricity from coal are examples of anthropogenic forcings.

How did we dodge a bullet with CFCs?

Before global warming and climate change were in the public eye, the world had to confront another anthropogenic crisis called the ozone hole. Baby boomers and their parents had all grown up believing chlorofluorocarbons (CFCs) were wonder chemicals that did no harm to anything, while keeping our food and ourselves cool. Suddenly, in the 1980s, we discovered CFCs were wolves in sheep's clothing and if we did not act quickly to get rid of them, atmospheric ozone would be gone and the sun's ultraviolet radiation would fricassee us. Most countries did act, and recent reports suggest that ozone levels are improving.

Fortunately, CFCs were made with chlorine. Had bromine been used, the ozone layer would have been destroyed before we had the tools to detect the damage.

How does "noise" complicate predictions of climate change?

Before scientists can accurately forecast what anthropogenic contributions to greenhouse gas in the atmosphere will do, they must consider random weather events called "noise." Noise might be an unusually strong storm, a warmer than average winter, or a cool summer brought on by the ash plume of a volcano. It might also be a huge weather pattern like El Niño.

In 1998 and 2005, the world had its two warmest years on record. 1998 featured an unusually strong El Niño, while 2005 did not. If the noise of El Niño's contribution of about 0.35°F (0.2°C) is factored out of the 1998 results, then 2002 through 2005 are the four warmest years on record.

What are aerosols?

In the world of weather, aerosols are particles in the atmosphere. They might be soot from cooking fires, dust from sandstorms, or ash from volcanoes. They might also be living things, swept up in a storm or sneezed by an animal. In large quantities, they can have a dramatic cooling effect on the Earth. Aerosols emitted as smoke from industries and automobiles are suspected of putting off our realization that global warming was happening by keeping the planet cooler than expected from 1940 to 1970, even though we were filling the air with carbon dioxide. Since then, efforts to reduce pollution and acid rain have also reduced our output of aerosols, making the effects of global warming gases like carbon dioxide and methane more noticeable.

Aerosols are extremely important in the development of clouds, rain, and snow because water vapour condenses on the particles.

Why are ice shelves collapsing on the Antarctic Peninsula?

Seven great chunks of ice, almost 7,000 square miles (11,300 square kilometres) in area and almost 700 feet (210 metres) thick, have broken off the Antarctic Peninsula since 1974. Climate scientists believe that temperature increases in the area of 4.5°F (2.5°C) during the last half-century are behind the breakup. The ice had been relatively stable in the area for the previous four hundred years.

According to climate change models, temperature changes of this magnitude at the poles are to be expected in response to overall global warming in the 1°F (0.6°C) range.

What is happening to the Yellow River?

Industrial pollution, losses to irrigation, masses of un-treated sewage, and fish die-offs are only part of the problem for China's second longest river. Much of the water for the 3,400-mile (5,500-kilometre) Yellow River comes from glaciers 15,000 feet (4,600 metres) above sea level on the Tibetan Plateau, and they are shrinking in the face of rising temperatures and a twenty-year drought. Is this climate change?

The river is used so heavily that it often dries up before it gets to the sea.

How is climate change affecting Mount Everest?

Although its exact height has always been subject to debate, Chinese scientists recently claimed that in their view, Everest is about 4 feet (1.2 metres) shorter than it was in 1975. They attribute this to anthropogenic global warming, based on analysis of ice cores from the mountain that indicate snow melt rates increased during the past century.

Khumbu Glacier, an important route up the mountain used by Sir Edmund Hillary and Tenzing Norgay during their ascent in 1953, has retreated three miles (five kilometres) since then.

How fast is Siberia's permafrost thawing?

Ground temperatures have risen by as much as 3°F (1.6°C) since the 1970s, and melt rates have accelerated to as much as eight inches (twenty centimetres) a year in some places. Across Siberia, thousands of lakes that once sat on permanently frozen ground are being absorbed into a swampy morass. In western Siberia, a huge 11,000-year-old peat bog is thawing, raising the possibility of a release of huge quantities of methane into the atmosphere, accelerating the buildup of greenhouse gases.

What is the Ward Hunt shelf?

At the northern end of Canada's Ellesmere Island, the Arctic's largest ice shelf split in 2002, three thousand years after it formed. The breakup followed a century of melting brought on by a warmer Arctic, which had seen the shelf lose almost 90 percent of its mass. When the ice split, a freshwater lake that sat on the denser saltwater of the Arctic Ocean drained away. Both the Ward Hunt shelf and the lake had provided habitat for specialized microscopic animals and plants.

Quickies

Did you know ...
- that in the north, global warming means snowmobile travel is more dangerous because the ice is unpredictable?
- that northern ice roads are useful for fewer days in the year?
- that melting permafrost causes roads to collapse?

How is China contributing to global warming?

China's production of greenhouse gases is growing at an alarming rate. In 1999, the country produced roughly half as much greenhouse gas as the United States. In 2006, its emissions almost equalled those of the U.S. The country is in the midst of a plan to build an estimated 1,000 megawatts (MW) of new coal-fired electrical generation every week until 2011, and a further 500 MW a week from 2012 to 2030. Given current rates of growth, its carbon dioxide emissions are on track to be double those of the U.S. by 2020.

Quickies

Did you know ...
- that, desperate for food, some wolves are threatening sled dogs tied up in Inuit communities?
- that western Hudson Bay polar bear populations have declined more than 20 percent since the early 1980s, because ice is breaking up earlier?
- that Emperor and Adelaide penguin populations are down considerably?
- that parasites, previously unknown in the far north, are killing reindeer?
- that black bears and beavers are being sighted further north in Alaska than ever before?
- that warming water in the Bering Sea is driving fish like pollock and pink salmon further north, and gray whales are following?
- that several species of shellfish once found in Monterey Bay, California, have moved north?
- that European butterfly populations, particularly those that specialize, are declining?

What is the IPCC?

The Intergovernmental Panel on Climate Change (IPCC) is a group of 2,500 scientists who have so far issued four reports on the state of the world's climate and projections of future changes. The panel's findings are highly politicized, because many countries are involved, so the publications avoid the extreme views on both sides of the issue. Nonetheless, the IPCC's first report in 1990 anticipated that a business as usual scenario would see a global temperature increase of about 5.4°F (3°C) by 2100. The fourth report in 2006 offered a worst-case scenario of 4.3°F to 11.5°F (2.4°C to 6.4°C) and a best-case of 2°F to 5.2°F (1.1°C to 2.9°C) by the end of this century.

The fourth report received widespread acceptance by governments around the world, which are now scrambling to put policies in place that will make the best-case scenario more likely.

Why are critics of global warming science falling silent?

Weather stations around the globe have been measuring temperature for almost 150 years with an ever-increasing number of devices on land and sea and in the air. Satellites entered the picture in the late 1970s, and soon after, discrepancies began to show up between their measurements and those taken on the surface of the Earth. The satellite data showed that warming was taking place, but much more slowly than expected, if models were correct. Critics of climate change theory seized upon these findings and used them to argue against major changes in public policy that would combat global warming. However, in the past few years, errors were found in the way the satellite data was calculated. Once these errors were corrected, measurements from satellites correlated much more closely with surface readings, adding validity to the predictions of climate change models.

What is happening to glaciers in Canada's Rockies?

The Athabasca Glacier, the best known glacier in North America, has retreated almost 1 mile (1.6 kilometres) in the last 125 years and has thinned and narrowed as well. It is one of six glaciers in the Columbia Icefield between Jasper and Banff, Alberta, and all are melting.

South of Banff, Glacier National Park in Montana is expected to soon be glacier free.

WEATHER MISCELLANY

What is the difference between El Niño and La Niña?

El Niño, "the boy" or "Christ child," is characterized by a warming of the western Pacific, which is most intense off the coast of Peru, and a cooling of the eastern Pacific off Indonesia. La Niña, "the girl," is just the opposite. They are the extreme ends of the El Niño/Southern Oscillation (ENSO), a naturally occurring cycle two to seven years long that varies in strength and has global consequences. El Niño events normally last about a year. La Niña can last three years.

What are extreme UV index readings?

Effects of an El Niño Phase

- Droughts and bush fires in Australia.
- Mild winters in Central Canada.
- Flooding and more avalanches in Western Canada.
- Famine and drought in Indonesia.
- Fewer, weaker hurricanes in the Atlantic.
- More, stronger tornadoes in the southern United States.
- Marine life and sea birds suffer around the Galapagos Islands, but life ashore is very good.
- Monsoon wind patterns change in the Indian Ocean.
- Drought in Austria.

Effects of a La Niña Phase

- Flooding in Australia, the Philippines, and Indonesia.
- Extreme cold in Alaska.
- Heavy rains, severe storms, and flooding in southern Africa.
- Drought in Kenya and Tanzania.
- Abnormal wetness in northern South America.
- Thriving marine life in the waters around the Galapagos, but suffering on land.
- Powerful storms battering California.

If the Earth was not protected by an ozone layer, UV index readings would top four hundred, and we would not be around to talk about them. For us, UV concentrations become dangerous when they exceed eleven, which they frequently do in the tropics. Canada's highest reading, 10.56, was taken in Toronto, in June 2005. At Mauna Loa Observatory in Hawaii, altitude 11,135 feet, readings in the twenties have been observed.

When did weather forecasting begin?

To avoid disaster, people have been trying to predict the weather for thousands of years, perhaps since the dawn of humankind, but their efforts were mostly self-serving until the telegraph came along and opened up the possibility of transmitting information across great distances nearly instantaneously. So it was not until the mid-1800s that attempts were made to start a weather service by Sir Francis Beaufort, creator of the Beaufort scale, and Robert Fitzroy, captain of the HMS *Beagle*, the ship that took Charles Darwin on the voyage that led to his famous book, *The Origin of Species*. Fitzroy made the first British weather forecast on August 1, 1861.

In the United States, limited weather forecasting began around 1860.

When did Canada start forecasting weather?

Canada began developing a weather service in 1871, and the first forecast took place in 1876. Statistical data started to appear at the end of the nineteenth century. Storm warnings were first issued in 1872.

Do You Know These Weather Rhymes?

- Mackerel sky, mackerel sky — never long wet, never long dry.
- Mare's tails; storms and gales.
- When clouds appear like rocks and towers, the Earth's refreshed with frequent showers.
- A little rain stills a great wind.
- If it's foggy in the morning then it'll be a sunny day.
- Rain before seven, clear by eleven.
- When dew is on the grass, no rain will come to pass.
- When halo rings the moon or sun, rain's approaching on the run.
- If the moon holds water it will be dry. If water from it can leak rain is nigh.
- When the glass falls low, stand by for a blow.
- Red sky at night, sailors delight. Red sky in the morning, sailors take warning.